The Children's Book of SAINTS

TEXT
Louis M. Savary, S.T.D.

ILLUSTRATIONS
Sheilah Beckett

MRP

THE REGINA PRESS
New York

THE REGINA PRESS
145 Sherwood Avenue
Farmingdale, New York 11735

ISBN: 0-88271-130-X

Cover and text illustration by Sheilah Beckett
Text designed and typeset by Roth Advertising

PRINTED IN BELGIUM

A Note to Parents and Teachers

Writing this book has given me new insights about being a Christian. As I wrote, I was impressed by some common characteristics of saints, which may be important for us to remember when sharing with children our faith in Christ.

First, *saints are not necessarily perfect people*. They usually have certain failures and weaknesses along with their good qualities. The important lesson they teach us is that we, too, can change and grow in our love for God and for each other. Thanks to God's grace, it is never too late to become a saint.

Second, *saints commonly give direct, caring service to others*. As a rule, saints have a strong sense of social justice. They seem to focus a lot of their attention and energy, as Jesus Himself did, on the poor, needy, uneducated, abused, and otherwise forgotten people of society.

Third, *saints on the whole seem to live lives that are filled with peace, joy, love, and energy*. It is simply not true that saints' lives are full of sadness, pain, and deprivation. Their joy and happiness, however, come from their love for God and for their fellow human beings.

In this book I have tried to select those saints that would be most attractive to American children. Eight of the saints qualify as American saints: Elizabeth Seton, Frances Cabrini, Isaac Jogues, John Neumann, Kateri Tekakwitha, Martin de Porres, Peter Claver, and Rose of Lima. Another eight have been named by the Church as special patrons of youth: Agnes, Aloysius, Cecilia, Dominic Savio, John Bosco, Maria Goretti, Stanislaus, and Therese, the Little Flower. In presenting the saints, I tended to emphasize, whenever possible, events from the saint's childhood or the saint's relationship to children.

Children are naturally God-centered, if properly guided. When exposed, but not coercively, to the devotional life of the church, children spontaneously show their innate capacity for prayer and service.

The prayers for each saint are written from the child's perspective. They are prayers a child can identify with easily. Speak often with your children about the saints, and pray the prayers together. These are the kind of memories that children never forget.

LOUIS M. SAVARY, S.T.D.

This book is dedicated to my father, who was always at my side in Church when I was a child.

Table of Contents

Mary, Queen of all Saints and Mother of Jesus, I know how much you love me. Let me come to you, Blessed Mother, to share all my joys and sorrows.

MARY, QUEEN OF SAINTS

Mary was an only child. She grew up loving God very much. Out of all women in history, God chose Mary to be the mother of His own Son, Jesus. When God's angel asked Mary if she would be the mother of Jesus, Mary answered yes.

As His mother, she was at Jesus' side when He was born in a stable in Bethlehem; she found Him when He was lost in the Temple at Jerusalem; she was with Him when He died on the cross on Calvary; and she was in the upper room to welcome Him when He rose from the dead on Easter.

In heaven, Mary was crowned Queen because she was mother of Jesus, mother of all the saints, and mother of the Church. That makes her our mother, too. Whenever we pray to Mary, we may call her mother, our Blessed Mother.

Saint Agnes, even as a young girl you were not afraid to die because you trusted in Jesus. Help me to love Jesus as fervently as you did.

SAINT AGNES

Agnes was only twelve years old when she was martyred for Christ. In those days, the Romans hated Christians, and soldiers were ordered to force Christians to worship the Roman gods.

For Agnes, to offer prayers and incense to Minerva would be to sin against God. So, instead of lighting the Roman incense, Agnes prayed aloud to Jesus in front of the soldiers.

They were so angry when Agnes did not obey that they handcuffed her, whipped her, and dragged her through the streets, hoping that people would laugh at her. But they did not. Instead, some tried to help her.

One young Roman offered to marry her so she would be protected. "It will save your life if you marry me," he said.

Agnes replied, "I belong to my Savior alone." At that, the angry soldiers killed her. She was truly a brave young woman.

Saint Aloysius, you studied hard, helped the sick, and loved Jesus and Mary with all your heart. Help me to be like you in your kindness and love.

SAINT ALOYSIUS GONZAGA

Aloysius Gonzaga was the son of a very noble Spanish family. His family expected him to marry and become a famous nobleman. But Aloysius was not interested in getting married or becoming famous. He loved God and Our Lady above all, and lived a very pure life.

At a young age, Aloysius joined the Society of Jesus. Among these young men, he was outstanding for the holiness of his life. He put aside all his expensive garments and wore only the cast-off clothing of others. He was also very brave.

When a terrible plague came upon Rome, Aloysius went out to care for the sick. He even brought home a very ill old man and took care of him in his own bed. Eventually, young Aloysius became sick and died in 1591.

He wanted very much to become a priest, but he did not live long enough. He is a patron saint of boys and girls.

$\mathcal{S}$aint Angela, even though you lived a comfortable life, you took the time to care for God's poor children. Help me to love the poor as you did.

SAINT ANGELA MERICI

Angela Merici was born in 1470, and was known in Italy as the friend of poor girls. Even though many of these poor girls had been born into Christian families, they were not taught anything about Jesus Christ and Our Lady. People told Angela these poor girls were no good, but she replied it was because no one had ever taught them how to be good. And Angela would teach them how.

When more and more poor young girls from the streets came to Angela, she decided she needed more help. She invited young women who were leading holy lives to help her. Many women joined her. They took Saint Ursula as their patroness and called their group the Ursuline Sisters. They built homes and schools all over the world to protect and teach poor girls. Today there are thousands of women who call themselves daughters of Saint Angela.

*S*aint Anne, mother of Our Lady and grandmother of Jesus, you never stopped praying. Help me when I feel discouraged and need hope.

SAINT ANNE

Anne is known to us because she is mother of Mary and grandmother of Jesus. Anne and her husband Joachim loved God and prayed for a child. It seemed God did not hear their prayers because years went by and a child never came. But they kept praying.

When it seemed Anne was too old to have a child, God gave them one. They called their special child Mary, a name which means incense that rises up to God. Anne's daughter became the woman that all Jewish women longed to be, the mother of the Messiah.

Anne was proud of Jesus. As His grandmother, she often had the opportunities to hold Him and play with Him. He often came to her house to visit.

Anne, whose name means "full of grace," was a holy woman who kept praying, even when it seemed useless to pray any longer.

Saint Anthony, you were asked by God to live your life in preaching and in caring for the needy. Help me to live for God and God's people.

SAINT ANTHONY OF PADUA

Statues or paintings of Saint Anthony often show him holding the Divine Child in his arms. That is because one night the Christ Child came to visit Anthony, kissed him, and told him how much He loved him.

Anthony often prayed that he would be a martyr. He wanted to die for love of Jesus. Instead, God asked him to live for the love of Jesus, and to work among the poor and the needy.

The Franciscan Order encouraged him to travel throughout Europe preaching the story of Jesus. The power of Jesus was so evident in everything Anthony did, that miracles happened. Small amounts of food multiplied to feed many people when Anthony blessed it. People with incurable diseases became well when Anthony touched them. People flocked to him, and children loved him. Everyone cried when the church bells announced that Anthony had died in the year 1231.

Saint Augustine, you can understand how people often turn away from goodness. Help those of us who sometimes find it difficult to be good.

SAINT AUGUSTINE

Augustine's story is that of a young man who was a sinner but who, by God's grace and his mother's prayers, became a wise and holy person. Augustine's mother Monica (who is also a saint) tried to make her son change his ways. "Make my son a good man," she begged God every day.

But clever and bright Augustine preferred not to be good. He fell in with bad company and led a wicked life. He was bright enough to know that what Christ taught was the truth, but he just did not want to be good.

One day, God's love and his mother's prayers finally won out, and Augustine decided to change his way of life. He became a priest and later was named a bishop. He used all his energy and intelligence to help the people of God. "Our hearts are made for You, O Lord," he once wrote, "and they are restless until they rest in You." He died in 430.

Saint Benedict, you lead people to God by the good example of your holy life. Help me learn to enjoy praying and working as you did.

SAINT BENEDICT

Benedict was born into a noble Roman family in 480, a time when there was evil and wickedness in the city. Men took delight in destroying buildings and terrifying people. When Benedict tried to be good, his schoolmates laughed at him. He decided he no longer wanted to live amid wickedness, so he ran away and hid in the mountains forty miles from Rome.

For the next three years, Benedict lived in a cave on the side of a cliff. Sometimes a raven brought him food to eat. Benedict had the power of miracles.

Young men who wanted to live good lives heard about Benedict. Many found their way to his mountain and asked if they could stay with him. Soon he had more than 140 companions. This was the beginning of the Benedictine Order. They built a house to live in, and remained there praying, planting crops, feeding the poor, and teaching school. Benedict's motto was "Pray and work."

Saint Bernadette, you were only a little child when Our Lady appeared to you. Help me to find Jesus and Our Lady in my own life.

SAINT BERNADETTE

On February 11, 1858 in Lourdes, France, Bernadette and her childhood friends went out to the fields to gather firewood. Her family was poor. While the others were playing games, Bernadette kept gathering wood. She came to a cave near a river, and saw a beautiful Lady dressed in blue and white, with stars around her head and roses at her feet.

When Bernadette told her family about the beautiful Lady, they did not believe her. But the Lady kept reappearing. One day the Lady told Bernadette to dig where she stood, and a fresh spring of water came bubbling out of the ground. Blind people who washed their faces in the spring could see. Sick people who washed their bodies in the water became well.

The Lady told Bernadette to build a great church there. This came to be known as the Shrine of Lourdes. Many miracles still happen there to this day.

$\mathcal{S}$aint Bridget, you prayed often to God, and your prayers moved you to action. Help me to be aware of the needs of those who are poor or sick.

SAINT BRIDGET OF SWEDEN

Bridget and her husband Ulf lived at the court of the Swedish King, Magnus II. She was the queen's special maid.

When Ulf died, Bridget lived a life of prayer and penance. King Magnus gave her money and land to build a monastery for a group of religious to be called the Order of the Holy Savior. In her monastery, people were not allowed to own anything but books.

Bridget traveled to Rome where she spent the rest of her life. Wherever she happened to be, she helped the poor and cared for the sick. She also spoke warnings to people who were leading evil lives.

People do not like to be told how bad they are, so Bridget was not well liked even though all recognized her holiness. She spent her life not only in prayer, but also in good works for the poor and the sick. Bridget died in 1373.

Saint Catherine Laboure, you loved Our Lady so much that she used you as an instrument to make many miracles happen. Help me to pray with faith and fervor.

SAINT CATHERINE LABOURE

Catherine was born on a farm in France in 1806. Her mother died when she was eight years old. Catherine walked miles each morning to attend daily Mass. Despite her father's reluctance, she became a Sister of the Daughters of Charity.

From childhood, Catherine experienced the presence of God and Our Lady in her prayer. In the convent, Our Lady appeared to her three times, telling her to have a holy medal made with the picture of Mary, the Immaculate Conception, stamped on it.

As soon as people began wearing the medal, miracles started happening. The medal soon began to be called the Miraculous Medal.

Catherine never told anyone but her confessor about the visions. So, even at her death in 1876, no one knew that Catherine was the one who brought the Miraculous Medal to the world.

Saint Catherine of Siena, you were brave in speaking for what you believed was right. Help me to stand up for my Church and for what is right.

SAINT CATHERINE OF SIENA

Catherine had a very important task in life. When she was a little girl, Jesus appeared to her. "Please give me your heart," He said.

When she offered Jesus her love, He gave her His Sacred Heart in return. Though many rich young men wanted to marry her, she chose instead to become a Dominican Sister.

At that time, Pope Gregory XI was living in exile in France. Catherine went to see him. She told him he should go back to Rome where his true home was. Because of Catherine, the Pope returned to Rome in 1376.

From that time on, the Pope and Catherine became friends. When things were not going well for the Church, Catherine encouraged the Pope to do something about it. He often took her advice. Catherine died in Rome in 1380.

People loved this fearless woman.

Saint Cecilia, patroness of music, help me to praise God with my life. Let my words and actions be like a song to God that says, "I love you."

SAINT CECILIA

Cecilia loved Jesus with all her heart and wanted to spend her whole life serving God. But she lived in Rome during the time when Christians were persecuted.

A young Roman nobleman wanted to marry her. When Cecilia said she belonged to God alone, the man and his brother tried to force her into marriage.

As the young man walked angrily toward Cecilia, he saw her guardian angel standing at her side. At this sight, the young man and his brother both became believers in Jesus.

The Roman soldiers took all three of them prisoners, and they were martyred.

Early in our century, Cecilia's body was found in its grave in Rome. Normally, buried bodies decay in a few years. But Cecilia's body was found to be fresh, sweet, and beautiful as if she were still asleep. Yet, she had been dead for eighteen hundred years.

Saint Clare, you exchanged the riches of a princess' life for the riches of Christ. Help me to know how good it is to love God with all my heart.

SAINT CLARE

Clare came from a wealthy and noble family in Assisi, and she desired to give herself totally to God. One day she heard Francis preaching in the streets. She felt Francis would understand her wish to serve God. The two of them became close friends, and they decided that Palm Sunday would be Clare's special day. At the time, she was eighteen years old.

On Palm Sunday, Clare dressed in beautiful clothes, and attended Mass with all the nobles. Even the bishop was there. That night, with a woman companion, Clare left the castle, and met Francis and his Brothers. At the altar of Our Lady in a chapel, Francis cut off her beautiful, long hair and Clare promised her life and love to Christ.

In an old house on the outskirts of town, Clare started an order of nuns which came to be known as the Poor Clares. They lived a life of prayer, silence, and fasting. Clare died in 1253.

Saint Dominic Savio, you found happiness in working hard to help other poor and homeless children. Show me how to be joyful in doing what I have to do.

SAINT DOMINIC SAVIO

Dominic, born in Italy in 1842, was only fifteen when he died. He had been a pupil of John Bosco, and grew up in his Home for Boys. Dominic had been a homeless child and John Bosco loved him as if he were his own son.

At an early age, Dominic organized a group of people called the Company of the Immaculate Conception to help John Bosco. Dominic's group was very poor, but they struggled together joyfully and worked hard to make the homes of John Bosco succeed.

Dominic wrote letters to his friends about his joy in helping poor and homeless children. In one letter he wrote, "Here we make holiness consist in being joyful all the time and in faithfully doing our duties."

Dominic is a model for young people who want to do important things for God.

Saint Elizabeth, even though you were a queen, you spent your life caring for the poor and the sick. Help me realize that God loves every human being.

SAINT ELIZABETH
OF HUNGARY

When Elizabeth was very young, she married Louis, a nobleman who became king. Elizabeth was kind to her husband and loved her children. She also felt that as a queen she should care for all of her people as if they were her own children. So, she welcomed the poor and the sick into her palace. When they could not come she went to visit them, carrying food in her cloak.

The king felt it was wrong for a queen to carry food as if she were a servant. One day he stopped her on her way to the hospital and asked to see what she was carrying in her cloak. When Elizabeth opened her cloak, dozens of red and white roses tumbled out. To her husband, the king, it was a sign that Elizabeth was a saint.

She died in 1231 when she was only twenty-four years old.

*S*aint Elizabeth Seton, you endured
sadness and misunderstanding from many
people. When I am sad or hurt, help me
to find comfort in knowing God loves me.

SAINT ELIZABETH SETON

There was much joy in the United States in 1975, for that was the year when Elizabeth Ann Seton was declared a saint. She was the first American saint to be born in the United States, but she was not born a Catholic. She was a convert.

In New York, where she lived, she opened a boarding school for children. Her husband had died, and this was the only way she had to support herself and her children. In 1805 when Elizabeth became a Catholic, St. Peter's was the only Catholic Church in New York City.

A priest encouraged Elizabeth to move to Baltimore and open a boarding school for Catholic girls, which she did. She and the women who helped run the new school wanted to become Sisters, so they started their own congregation called the Daughters of Charity in 1809.

Saint Frances Xavier Cabrini, you always said that God did everything. Help me to trust that God cares for me and what I am trying to do.

SAINT FRANCES
XAVIER CABRINI

Frances Cabrini was born in Italy, in 1850, but America claims her as a saint because Mother Cabrini became an American citizen in 1909.

Her life was filled with difficulties and setbacks. In Italy, she tried to enter several religious communities, but they all refused to accept her because her health was poor. When she began working with five other women at an orphanage in Italy, the bishop closed the orphanage. Next she asked the Pope if she and her companions could go to China as missionaries. He said no, and sent her instead to the United States. When she arrived in New York, the bishop advised her to return to Italy.

However, she remained in New York, opened orphanages and schools, and began a small hospital. She and her companions founded the Missionary Sisters of the Sacred Heart.

S aint Francis of Assisi, you showed us how God created all people, animals, and plants to live together in unity. Help me to love all creatures God made.

SAINT FRANCIS OF ASSISI

As a young man, Francis was very wealthy and enjoyed the pleasures of life. But once when he was sick, he felt that God was calling him to live as Jesus did. Francis responded to God's call and began to visit the sick in hospitals and to do helpful things for the poor. "When people serve the poor," Francis said, "they are serving Christ Himself."

Francis began to wear clothes like the poor, and he started to preach to people about peace and unity. "All the things God created are like our brothers and sisters," he said. Francis often addressed the sun, moon, stars, and animals as brother or sister.

Once during prayer Francis had a vision of Jesus hanging on the cross. So deep was Francis' desire to be like his Lord, that the marks of Jesus' five wounds appeared in Francis' body and remained there all his life. He died in 1226.

Saint Francis de Sales, you spent your life with the words of Jesus on your lips. Help me always to use Jesus' name with reverence and love.

SAINT FRANCIS DE SALES

Francis was born in France in 1567. It seemed God had destined him to have a special task in the Church from his childhood. This task was to teach and write the truth about Jesus so that everyone would understand.

In school, Francis spent many years studying difficult subjects like philosophy, theology, and law. He became a lawyer, and one day heard a voice saying to him, "Leave all and follow me." So, he became a priest and went to help the poor and sinners.

Even after he became the bishop of Geneva and had many duties caring for his people, he still continued to teach.

He found time to write many books, some of which are still famous. In one, called *Introduction to the Devout Life*, he showed how people living ordinary lives can become saints.

$\int$aint Francis Xavier, you rejoiced in all the skills and gifts God gave you. Help me to enjoy using my talents for God and to love God with all my heart.

SAINT FRANCIS XAVIER

Francis Xavier was named Patron of the Missions, and was considered the greatest missionary since Saint Paul. Actually, Francis was great at many things. In Spain, as a youth, he was a great athlete, a champion runner, and the leader in his class at school. He was also a true friend to those who knew him. However, he was greatest at loving God.

At the University of Paris, when Francis was winning all the prizes in school, he met Ignatius Loyola. They became life-long friends, and helped start the Society of Jesus. Ignatius once asked Francis, "What good will it do if you win all the prizes in the world, but lose your soul?"

"Send me out as a missionary," Francis replied, "and I will win the whole world for our dear Lord." Francis spent the rest of his life preaching Christ and baptizing among the peoples of India and Japan. He died in 1552.

$\mathcal{S}$aint Gemma, you learned to experience Jesus' own joy and suffering in your prayer. Help me to know Jesus more closely and more lovingly.

SAINT GEMMA GALGANI

Gemma lived in Italy about one hundred years ago. She was a pious girl and wanted to become a Passionist nun, but was refused permission because of ill health. In fact, she soon caught tuberculosis, and doctors pronounced her incurable. However, Gemma's faith was so strong—she prayed to Saint Gabriel—that she was completely cured.

As soon as she was healthy, she reapplied to the Passionists, but again they refused to have her. So, Gemma continued to live her devout life at home.

The priests who directed her spiritual life spoke to others of Gemma's many ecstasies and visions. The marks of Jesus' crucifixion appeared on her hands and feet many times over a period of two years.

As a single woman, she lived the life of a mystic, very close to God. She was hailed as a saint long before her death in 1903.

Saint George, you understand how much courage is needed to deal with evil in life. Help me to love Christ and to be courageous like you.

SAINT GEORGE

We know very little about George, except that he was a soldier and a holy man. He is often pictured in combat with a dragon. If we think of the dragon as a symbol of evil in our lives, then Saint George can be our helper whenever we have to do battle with our dragons.

George began as a soldier in the Roman Army, but rose to a high rank because of his bravery. When George became a Christian, he left the army. When the Roman Emperor published an edict persecuting Christians, George is said to have torn it down. He was martyred for his faith in Christ around the year 303.

Among the Greeks, George is called "the great martyr," and his feast is kept as a holy day in Greece.

The people of England liked George so much that they chose him to be their patron saint. He is also the patron of Boy Scouts.

Saint Helen, you searched for the true Cross of Jesus and in that sign your son made the world a safe place for Christians. Help me to find strength in Jesus' Cross.

SAINT HELEN, EMPRESS

Helen began her life as a British princess, but through marriage she became Empress of Rome. Even though she was not a Christian then, she was a good woman. Because of her kindness, God gave her the gift of belief in Jesus.

Helen was concerned about finding the Cross on which Jesus had died. At eighty years of age, she went to Jerusalem to search for it. She found three crosses together, but could not tell which one was the true Cross. Then a sick woman came by, and when she touched the true Cross she was healed.

Constantine, Helen's most powerful son, was not a Christian. After hearing the story about the true Cross, Constantine said that if he won his next battle he would become a Christian. He won and then used the Cross as his symbol. He became the first Christian ruler in the world.

Saint Ignatius, you read about the saints and wanted to do what they did for God. Help me to be the saint that I can be.

SAINT IGNATIUS LOYOLA

In 1521, Ignatius Loyola, the soldier, had his knee wounded in battle. While he was recovering from his wound, he began reading about Christ and the saints. "I can do what they did," he said to himself. Ignatius pictured the world as a battlefield. So he decided to become a "soldier of Christ."

While at the University of Paris, Ignatius began to gather friends who wanted to serve with him under the banner of Christ. These young men called themselves the Companions of Jesus. People nicknamed them the Jesuits, and the order was known as the Society of Jesus.

"The Companions," Ignatius said, "are ready to do any work or go anywhere in the world for God's greater glory."

The Jesuits became famous as teachers and missionaries. Amid all their fame, they chose to live among the poor and to teach catechism to children.

Saint Isaac Jogues, you were a man of great faith and heroism. Help me find ways to tell people how much God loves them.

SAINT ISAAC JOGUES

Isaac Jogues was one of eight Jesuits from France who came to America to bring the teachings of Christ to the Indians. Isaac was ordained a priest in 1636, and was soon sent to Canada to do missionary work among the Huron Indians.

The peaceful Hurons were often attacked by the warlike Iroquois tribe. During an attack, Isaac and many of the Hurons were captured, tortured, and beaten. Isaac escaped to New York, and boarded a ship back to France.

He soon returned to the New World to resume his missionary work among the Hurons. On his way, however, he was captured by a Mohawk war party and beheaded in 1646.

All of the eight Jesuit companions were martyred by Indians in the New World. They wanted to teach the Indians of God's love, even at the cost of their own lives.

Saint Isidore, you loved the earth which gives us food and the God who gave us the earth. Help me to be like you in sharing food with the hungry.

SAINT ISIDORE, THE FARMER

People all over the world love this Spanish saint, especially farmers and those who live in rural communities. Isidore is the patron saint of farmers, and people ask his intercession for rain, good weather, and good crops.

Isidore was born in Madrid and had very little education. From his youth, he worked on a farm as a hired hand. As he walked behind the plow, he prayed. He said that everything reminded him of God. He had a great reverence for animals and never let them be mistreated.

He went to Mass faithfully every morning. God sent his angels to make up for the work Isidore missed while at Mass.

When Isidore saw poor people, he brought them food, prayed with them, and encouraged them to trust in God.

Isidore's life reminds us that even very ordinary people can become saints. He died in 1130.

Saint Jane Frances, you spent your whole life teaching children to love and serve God. Teach me how to pray and show my love to God.

SAINT JANE FRANCES DE CHANTAL

Jane showed us that a woman can be holy in many roles. Jane was holy as a child, holy as a wife, holy as a widow, and holy as a religious sister.

As a child, Jane asked Our Lady to take care of her. Jane was blessed with a wealthy husband and many children, but sadness struck. Because of sickness, she lost her husband, as well as two of her children and her own sister. People told her to marry again. "It will make you happy," they said. But Jane remained a widow and brought up the rest of her family.

When her children were grown and on their own, Jane felt a desire to become a nun. In 1610, Saint Frances de Sales helped her found a new order called the Visitation Sisters. There are many such sisters in the world today.

Saint Joan of Arc, God called you from your simple life as a shepherdess to lead a nation to freedom. Help me to be brave and respond to God's call.

SAINT JOAN OF ARC

Joan of Arc was a shepherdess who lived a quiet life with her simple family. At that time, her homeland France was being overrun by British soldiers.

As Joan prayed for the freedom of her homeland and the safety of the French soldiers, she began hearing God's voice telling her to go and save her country.

At first, she could not believe God could be asking her to wear armor and ride a horse into battle. Yet the voices continued to urge her, so she lead the fearful French soldiers on to victory. Then she herself crowned Charles VII King of France in his palace at Rheims.

When the king was crowned, Joan asked to be allowed to return to her family, but the king refused. In 1431 some of the jealous soldiers turned her over to the enemy who burned her to death.

$\mathcal{S}$aint John the Baptist, you pointed out Jesus to those who came to you. Help me to recognize Jesus in all the ways He comes into my life.

SAINT JOHN THE BAPTIST

Before John was born, an angel had announced, "Many will rejoice at his birth."

John's mother Elizabeth and Our Lady were first cousins, so Jesus and John were second cousins. John, who was six months older than Jesus, lived in a suburb of the Holy City, Jerusalem.

When they were children, Jesus and John probably visited each other and played together. They both grew up learning about the Temple in Jerusalem and the Holy Law.

When they were about thirty years old, John began preaching near the Jordan River, and baptizing those who repented. Jesus was among those who came to be baptized.

John had the special task of recognizing Jesus when He came. John told his own disciples to follow Jesus because Jesus was much more important than he was.

John was later beheaded by King Herod.

Saint John Baptist de la Salle, you had a special concern to provide good and holy teachers for children. Help me to learn from all who teach me.

SAINT JOHN BAPTIST
DE LA SALLE

John Baptist de la Salle was born in 1651, and is the patron saint of teachers. He wanted to help the badly educated poor children in France. So, with a group of others, he began to help out in a school where the teachers gave their services free of charge. John gave away all his money to the needy, and founded an institute of teachers we call the Christian Brothers. Not only did they provide free schools, but John created new kinds of schools called high schools and technical schools where children could learn a trade.

Since John realized that children often needed special help in learning, he began the first training colleges for teachers. In this way, he prepared a large number of teachers to teach children well.

John told these teachers they should love their pupils as a parent would, and to give all their time and energies to them.

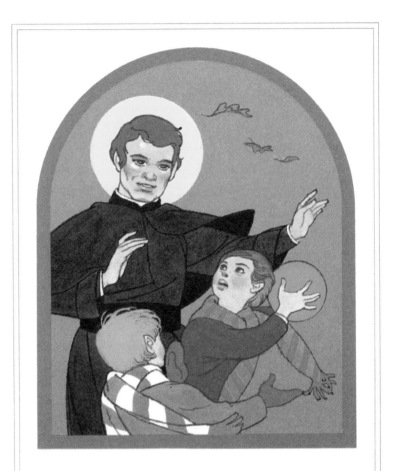

Saint John Bosco, you dedicated your life to the care of children. Help me when I pray to Jesus and help me to pray lovingly with my friends.

SAINT JOHN BOSCO

John Bosco was a poor Italian shepherd boy who wanted to become a priest. When his mother first saw him dressed in clerical robes in the seminary, she was proud of him. However, she told him to remember that priests honor God not only by wearing clerical clothing, but by following the way of His Son.

John remembered what his mother said, and lived a life of which his mother would be proud. His life work was caring for young boys and girls. For this, he is called the Apostle of Youth.

About 1860, he founded the Salesian Society which offered shelter to homeless children and taught them useful skills and trades. He also taught them about their Catholic faith, and stressed their spiritual development. Even though his motto was, "Give me only souls and keep all the rest," John Bosco cared for the whole child—body, mind, and spirit.

Saint John Neumann, you taught many children to know and love God. Help me to understand my faith and to talk joyfully about God.

SAINT JOHN NEUMANN

Although John Neumann was born in 1811 in Europe, he came to New York to be ordained a priest. His first assignment was to work among the immigrants in Buffalo. Because he knew seven languages fluently, he could speak about God to many people in their native language. He was a hard worker, visited the sick, comforted the needy, and trained teachers.

He was appointed Bishop of Philadelphia in 1852. When he arrived there, he found only two Catholic schools for children. Within eight years, he opened almost a hundred more. Even though he was a bishop, he still would teach class because he loved children.

John helped the church in the United States grow and prosper. He wrote two catechisms, a Bible history, and a handbook for priests.

John Neumann followed Christ's command to "Go and teach all nations."

Saint Joseph, husband of Mary, you were always aware of God's presence. Help me find God in my life, and be with me at the hour of my death.

SAINT JOSEPH

Joseph was a quiet, hardworking carpenter who kept God's commandments. He loved Mary and wanted to marry her. She agreed, but when Joseph saw that Mary was going to have a baby and it was not his, be became very upset.

In a dream, God's angel told Joseph it was all right to marry Mary. The angel explained how the baby was God's own baby, and Joseph was being given the sacred task of protecting and supporting Mary and the baby Jesus.

Joseph listened to his dream, accepted the task, and became the foster-father of Jesus. Joseph loved Jesus very much, and taught him all he knew about carpentry. Jesus spent many years working with Joseph.

We are told that when Joseph died, Jesus and Mary were present and he died a happy death. Saint Joseph is the patron saint of a happy death.

$\int$aint Jude, you were open to the Holy Spirit's loving energy. Help me to trust in God's care and to come to you when things seem hopeless.

SAINT JUDE

Jude, also called Thaddeus, was one of the twelve apostles, and probably a first cousin of Jesus. He was a very quiet and humble man.

He is often pictured with the flame of the Holy Spirit touching his head. God's spirit at Pentecost so filled Jude with the love of God that he wanted to tell all people about that love.

After Jesus' Ascension, Jude traveled as a missionary to Syria and Mesopotamia. Wherever he went, he taught people to be simple, humble, and prayerful. He made many converts, especially among the Jewish people living in those countries. He sent a long letter to his Jewish Christian friends. "We owe God praise and thanksgiving for His endless mercy," he wrote.

Jude is the special patron of the sick, especially those who are hopeless cases.

$\int$aint Kateri, you lived a life of peace and penance among warlike people. Inspire me to be fervent in prayer and to put my trust in God.

SAINT KATERI TEKAKWITHA

Saint Kateri is truly an American saint. The Mohawk Indian Tribe from which she came walked the plains and mountains of North America long before Columbus' boats first reached the New World.

Kateri did not hear about Christ until Christian missionaries came to New York and Canada. Although many Mohawks were cruel to the missionaries, Kateri listened to their words and felt a call to be baptized a Christian.

Kateri resolved to remain a virgin and to spend her life in prayer. She supported and encouraged the Christian missionaries. They called her "Lily of the Mohawks" and were inspired by her devotion to the Blessed Sacrament. The Rosary was one of her favorite forms of prayer. She did much penance to make reparation to God for the cruelty of the Indians and European settlers toward each other. Kateri died in 1680.

Saint Lucy, you loved God with all your heart. Help me to have great faith so that I can help sick people get well through my prayers, as you did.

SAINT LUCY

When Lucy was a little girl, her mother became very sick. "Don't worry," Lucy told her mother, "I will pray for you and you will get well." Lucy walked to the little church of Saint Agatha in Rome and prayed.

Saint Agatha appeared to her and called her, "My sister." (We are all sisters and brothers in Christ's family.) Agatha promised Lucy that her mother would get well. She also told Lucy that she would die a martyr for Christ.

Lucy's mother got well the very next day, but there was no sign of any threat to Lucy's life.

Some years later, Lucy became a nun. This angered the young Roman who wanted to marry her, so he told the authorities persecuting the Christians that Lucy was secretly a nun. The soldiers seized her and put her to death. She went to heaven to be with God.

$\mathcal{S}$aint Margaret Mary, you loved the Sacred Heart with all your heart. Help me to make up for some of the cruelty in the world by my strong love.

SAINT MARGARET MARY

We call Jesus "The Sacred Heart" because of His great love for us. The woman who did more than anyone else to make the Sacred Heart known was named Margaret Mary. She was born in France in 1647.

Margaret Mary was a sister who loved God with all her heart. Because she was sorry that everyone did not love Jesus, she often knelt for hours in a chapel before the tabernacle. The tabernacle contained the communion host, which we call the Blessed Sacrament.

One day as she was praying, Jesus appeared and showed her His Sacred Heart. "Behold the Heart that has loved humans so much," He said. "Tell others about My love for them."

Sister Margaret Mary spent the rest of her life telling people about the promises the Sacred Heart made to those who love Him.

 S aint Maria, you would not allow your
body to be used in an evil way. Help me
to treat my body as a temple of God.

SAINT MARIA GORETTI

Maria Goretti, a patron saint of youth, was born on a farm in Italy in 1890. Her mother described Maria as happy, open-hearted, and never disobedient. Maria's father died when she was nine, so she learned to watch the children and do housework, while her mother ran the farm.

When Maria was eleven years old, a neighbor's teenage boy, Alexander, made advances at her with evil intentions. She refused, but never told her mother about the incident. Alexander continued his advances, and she continued to resist. But one day in anger he attacked her with a knife and mortally wounded her.

Dying in the hospital, Maria forgave Alexander and wished that some day he would be in heaven. Her prayer was answered. Though Alexander led an evil life for many years, he eventually repented and became a Capuchin brother. He lived to see Maria canonized a saint.

Saint Martin de Porres, you spent your life in service to the sick and the poor. Help me to be aware when people need me.

SAINT MARTIN DE PORRES

Martin was born in Peru in 1579. His father was a Spanish knight and his mother a free black woman from Panama. Martin's mother sent him to study medicine. He used what he learned to care for the sick in the poor section of town where he was welcome as a black man.

He joined the Dominican Order in Lima, Peru. At first, because he was black, he suffered many insults, even from his fellow monks. But his kindness and holiness won the monks over, and they flocked to him. He would sit and pray with them when they were worried, and would tend them when they were sick.

So many people of the town began to come to Martin with their illnesses, that he turned homes into hospitals. He also opened orphanages, begging on the streets for money and food to care for these abandoned children.

All the people of Lima loved him.

Saint Patrick, you loved to make people happy by telling wonderful stories about God. Help me to be able to tell others how much God loves us.

SAINT PATRICK

Patrick was born somewhere in Europe, but he developed a special love for the people of Ireland. In those days, the Irish did not know about Jesus and Mary. Patrick wanted to tell them, so the Pope sent Bishop Patrick to Ireland.

Because Patrick was a very likable person, the Irish people welcomed him. They loved stories and song, and they especially loved the stories Patrick told them about Jesus and Mary. He taught the Christian faith in story form. For example, he explained the Holy Trinity by pointing to the shamrock flower which had three leaves yet was one plant.

The kings and soldiers sat and listened to him, as did the women. All asked to be baptized. Patrick traveled through Ireland preaching the Christian religion. The Irish people have always remained faithful to the heritage brought by Patrick. He died about 461.

Saint Paul, you were an apostle of Christ and a missionary to foreign countries. Help my heart to burn with love for Jesus and for all His people.

SAINT PAUL

Before Paul met Jesus, he had been called Saul. He was a short man, full of energy and emotion. He always acted with great intensity and held his beliefs very strongly.

At first he hated Jesus and persecuted Christians. One day, riding on a horse, he was knocked to the ground by what seemed like a lightening bolt.

During the next few days he began to believe in Jesus, was baptized, and his name was changed to Paul. He went from city to city telling everyone that Jesus is Lord.

Wherever Paul went, he started new communities of Christians. He treated each community like a large family that belonged to Jesus. Paul's love for Jesus was like a fire that burned in his heart. In Rome, Paul's enemies put him in prison, where he died about the year 67.

 Saint Peter, first among all the apostles, you showed how even a strong person can be weak. Help us ask Jesus for forgiveness whenever we deny the truth.

SAINT PETER

Simon was an expert fisherman. He was also a powerful person, but sometimes his temper flared. Jesus chose him to lead His apostles when He changed his name and said, "You are Peter and on this rock I will build my Church."

Jesus preached from Peter's fishing boat, and cured Peter's mother-in-law when she was sick. Jesus took Peter with Him wherever He went.

Peter had his weaknesses. When things became difficult, Peter might talk bravely, but he did not always act so. When Jesus was put on trial, Peter did not go into court but stayed out in the yard. When one of the women there asked Peter if he was a follower of Jesus, Peter denied it. He lied to save himself. Immediately, Peter was sorry, and Jesus forgave him.

At Pentecost, God sent the Holy Spirit into Peter, and Peter was never afraid to tell the truth again.

$\mathcal{S}$aint Peter Claver, you had a special love for people who were treated as slaves. Help me to realize that God loves every human being.

SAINT PETER CLAVER

Peter Claver, a Jesuit priest, dedicated himself by a special vow to the service of African slaves. He worked in what is today Colombia, South America. At that time, it was the biggest slave market in the New World. It was said that a thousand slaves arrived there every month.

Peter would climb aboard the slave ships as they docked, and offer the slaves whatever food or drink he had. He would care for the sick and the dying.

By means of native interpreters, he would teach the slaves about Jesus Christ. He baptized more than three hundred thousand slaves in his lifetime. He also visited his new Christians when they were taken to plantations to work. He encouraged the masters to treat them humanely, and he fought to abolish the African slave trade. Peter had remarkable energy and patience to work under these conditions. He died in 1654.

Saint Rose, through prayer and love you developed your true beauty. Help fill my life with the love and beauty that comes from God.

SAINT ROSE OF LIMA

Rose is an American saint. She was born in Lima, Peru less than one hundred years after Columbus discovered America. At baptism, her parents gave her the name Isabel, but people called her Rose because she was very beautiful.

Rose was so afraid her beauty would lead her into evil ways that she cut off her hair, worked until her hands became rough, and wore ugly clothing.

All around her, people were leading evil lives, and she wanted to make up for their sins. She wanted God to know how much she loved Him, so she did penance for the sins of others. She lived in a little hut and slept on the dirt floor.

She became a Dominican nun, and was known for her power of prayer. The people loved her, and to this day they claim her prayers drove away an enemy fleet that was attacking Peru.

*S*aint Stanislaus, you had a great love for Jesus in holy communion. Help me to reverence this sacred food and to receive Jesus often in holy communion.

SAINT STANISLAUS KOSTKA

Stanislaus was brought up in the Polish Court. His family was very wealthy and considered noble. Stanislaus was deeply prayerful and pure. At mealtimes, when men used vulgar and dirty language, he became embarrassed and left the table.

He and his brother were sent off to boarding school together, but his brother bullied him so badly that Stanislaus ran away. When his brother chased him on horseback, intending to punish him and bring him back, God let Stanislaus be invisible to his brother as he rode by.

Cold and frightened, Stanislaus came to an empty church. He wished he could have holy communion to give him courage, but there was no priest there. Then an angel came and gave him communion.

Stanislaus walked many hundred miles to Vienna where he joined the Society of Jesus. He died a very young man in 1568. He is a patron saint of youth.

Saint Stephen, you were able to forgive your enemies who were angry at you.
Help me to understand those who get
angry at me and treat them lovingly.

SAINT STEPHEN

Stephen became one of the first permanent deacons in the Church. He and six others were ordained deacons by Jesus' first Apostles. The deacon's task was to live a holy life and to help care for the poor in the Christian community.

Stephen also had a gift for teaching and doing wonders. Because of his powerful preaching about Jesus, some of the Jews became angered and brought him before the Jewish court. Standing in front of everyone, Stephen spoke bravely and with great wisdom. People said a halo appeared around Stephen's head, and his face looked angelic.

When Stephen said, "I see the heavens opened and the Son of Man standing at the right hand of God," an angry crowd dragged him outside the city and stoned him to death. As Stephen was dying, he asked God to forgive his enemies. Stephen was the first martyr for Jesus.

Saint Therese, you wanted only to love God, but you helped many people at the same time. Help prayer to be easier when I find it difficult.

SAINT THERESE, THE LITTLE FLOWER

Therese Martin was born in Alencon, France in 1873. From her earliest days, Therese told her father she wanted to belong totally to God. "You are too young to be a religious sister," he said.

Therese then asked the Pope for special permission. He said it would be all right, and so she entered the French Carmelites at the age of 15.

"I just want to love God," she said to the sisters. Therese was a simple girl and wanted to find easy ways to pray. "People are creating wonderful inventions to make things easier," she said. "I would like to invent a prayer elevator to God."

She is often called the Little Flower because she promised, "After I die, I will drop down from heaven a shower of roses." And that is just what she did. Many miracles have happened because of her.

Saint Thomas, the Apostle, you doubted Jesus but were not afraid to speak; your doubt brought Jesus to you. Help me not to be afraid of having doubts.

SAINT THOMAS, THE APOSTLE

Thomas was one of Jesus' twelve Apostles. He was very impulsive. Sometimes his quickness got him in trouble, sometimes it brought special blessings from Jesus. Once he bravely said he was willing to court danger and even death just to be with Jesus.

Thomas was also a doubter. When the other Apostles told Thomas they had seen the risen Lord on the first Easter, he doubted. "Unless I see the nail imprint in His hands and put my finger there," Thomas said, "I will not believe." So Jesus came back a second time to prove to Thomas that He had indeed risen from the dead. When he saw Jesus, Thomas had no more doubts.

After Jesus ascended to heaven, Thomas journeyed to the East as a missionary, passing through Persia and going to India. Some believers in India still call themselves Christians of Saint Thomas.

Saint Thomas Aquinas, you were both brilliant and holy. Help me with my studies and help me to become a holy person.

SAINT THOMAS AQUINAS

Thomas Aquinas always wanted to be a priest, but his family tried to stop him. He wanted to preach and teach as Saint Dominic had done. About 1245, when Thomas went to live with the Dominicans, his two brothers brought him back and locked him in their castle for almost two years. The Pope himself heard about Thomas and commanded his family not to stand in his way.

Thomas was very wise and also very holy. In Latin, his nickname was *Doctor Angelicus*, which means the teacher who is like an angel.

Thomas wrote the most famous theology books of all time. All priests and seminarians study his books.

Thomas also wrote beautiful poems and music. We still sing some of his songs in Church. When God asked Thomas what reward he wanted, Thomas said, "Lord, I want only You." He died in 1274.

Saint Thomas More, you knew how to praise God and still be happy. Help me to be cheerful throughout life, and to make as little wrong as possible.

SAINT THOMAS MORE

"Praise God and be merry!" was one of Thomas More's favorite sayings. He did not believe holy people had to remain by themselves, or look sad. Thomas was a cheerful man, who loved to spend time with his friends, especially at a party.

He raised a large family, and even adopted several children. In a time when girls were kept in the kitchen, he believed girls should be as well educated as boys, and did so with his own daughters.

Thomas wisely realized there were always going to be wicked people in the world and we would frequently have to deal with them. So he wrote to his friends, "Handle everything as gently as you can. And what you cannot put right, you must try to make as little wrong as possible."

Thomas was beheaded in 1535 by King Henry VIII because he would not compromise his Christian beliefs. He is the patron of lawyers.

Saint Vincent de Paul, you happily spent your life giving everything you had to God's poor. Help me to realize that God loves me when I give cheerfully.

SAINT VINCENT DE PAUL

Vincent de Paul was a priest who was most remembered for his kindness. "Give" was the word that described his daily life. He worked to earn money, then gave it all away to the poor. He brought poor people who were sick to his own home and cared for them. He is the patron of charitable societies.

Poor children were always hanging on his coattails. To them, he gave food, clothing, toys, and all the love that was in his heart.

To help his work with the poor, Vincent gathered a group of men and women dedicated to God. The women, who called themselves Sisters of Charity, nursed the sick and cooked meals for them. The men with Vincent, who called themselves Priests of the Mission, collected food and clothes for those who could not work. After his death in 1660, the Vincentians and the Sisters of Charity continued the work Vincent had started.

ALL SAINTS DAY

Besides the saints described in this book, there are hundreds of other saints whose names are listed in the Church's canon of saints, and millions of other saints in heaven whose names are known only to God. That is why we celebrate a day for all the saints.

What does it mean to be a saint? To be proclaimed a saint by the Church has a lot of special requirements. To be a saint in God's eyes—which is more important anyway—is a lot easier. As long as you believe in Jesus and are trying to live a life that is pleasing to God and loving toward others, God says you qualify as a saint, that is, you belong to the Communion of Saints.

You are probably a saint right now. I hope you will remain among the Communion of Saints forever.